What Came After

Poems

Christopher Stewart

2024 The Calliope Group, LLC

Published in the United States by The Calliope Group, LLC
Tulsa, Oklahoma

ISBN: 979-8-9866015-4-0 (Trade Paperback)
ISBN: 978-1-7336474-5-7 (eBook)

Library of Congress Control Number: 2023949770

ACKNOWLEDGEMENTS

Grateful acknowledgment is made to the editors of the following publications in which these works or earlier versions of them previously appeared:

Oakwood
The Perch
After Hours
Bryant Literary Review
Connecticut River Review
Deronda Review
Red Shoes Review
Red Truck Review
San Diego Poetry Annual 2022- 2023
The Walmart Republic/Mongrel Empire Press

Praise for *What Came After*

"*What Came After* offers a searing series of poems that explore, in exquisitely human and intimate detail, the struggles associated with mental illness. *Daybreak arrives in the shape of a gun*, opens the poem Clinical, Part II. The line is applicable to the book as a whole: that stark but nagging contrast between darkness and tainted light; the quiet desperation and tender screams of interior violence made exterior, made flesh. From Dallas to San Francisco to Chicago, from a post-Kennedy/King birth to an unsettled, polarized now, Stewart's lush lyricism reminds us we are linked by a tether of dim hope. These poems are a reckoning with ache, memory and self, grounded in the heavy empathy of the shared moment and the relative distance of time."—Quraysh Ali Lansana, author of t*he skin of dreams: new and collected poems 1995-2018* and *Opal's Greenwood Oasis.*

"*What Came After* offers no answers, just the sure-handed telling of a life that has included mental illness, abuse, and loss but also kindness, comfort, and intimacy. Without smoothing the harsh or overlooking the tender, Christopher Stewart creates a stunning urgency in each of these poems. Throughout this excellent new collection, Stewart demonstrates a deft use of detail, often understated, that both pierces the heart and jolts the reader awake. I highly recommend this book."—Mike Puican, author of *Central Air.*

"'The years reveal a tally of losses…' These opening words of *What Came After* are part of a gravitational pull towards something unlikely — discovery at every turn. Christopher Stewart gives us language that is inventive, edifying, and out of the ordinary. The poet tells American stories that are personal and communal, made of memory, both brutal and brave."—Michael Warr, Poetry Editor, *Of Poetry & Protest From Emmett Till to Trayvon Martin*

For my siblings: Charles, Charlotte, Cathryn, Suzy, Cindy, and Robert. We are still here.

And for Q, who knows why.

CONTENTS

III.

IV.

This is my letter to the World
That never wrote to Me

Emily Dickinson

I

What Came After

The years reveal a tally of losses:
recoiling from a lover's lips on our thighs,
begging for manhood in moments
when beauty and unencumbered desire
were offered freely. The body's engine
coughs, sputtering refusals.

This occurs in time but is free of time,
the way the body stores a memory: a scent
(the way his hands smelled like engine oil)
or a parcel of a phrase spoken
decades ago you still hear.

Though they are owed an inestimable debt,
the boys who were with me in that house,
who weathered that suffering season when
his carnal breath was hot on our slim necks
whispering his pleasures in our shame
know some things can never be reclaimed.
Our past became a charnel house of memory
shaping the bony present.

We rejoined body and soul at dented seams
by learning the raveled language of mercy.
Praise songs and doxologies of our own.
Despite our still unsteady voices, rising
like wonders into the ashy rafters.

Being Good

In Kelly Park, a little boy wraps his arms
around his mother's legs as two girls run
for his hill. The look in his eyes
is part fear, part curiosity. For his mother,
it is one of those moments that shape
the collective sum of things, an image
of many she may recall: an afternoon
in late September, her tremulous boy
holding on to the oak of her as she looks
across the dinner table at him years later.
He has gone to Stanford. He is an engineer.

And so it is with memory, arriving
in an instant like this. His lank fingers
down the front of my sweatpants.
His mustache, smelling of fried eggs
and nicotine pressed against my neck.
Everything about him was old, yet sheen,
viscous like something dredged
from a dirty river that snakes slag fields
carrying coal barges down to the sea.

Another boy was there. While I have
not spoken to him in years, I want to
warn him one can trace a lifetime
of cowardice to a single moment.
That we must be careful of autumn
in our middle years, when images
conflate into things we dare not see
in a treeless place, with me.

Leaving Klonopin

How long has it been, old friend? I recall
an airport bar, my third Makers Mark, you
cradled in a cocktail napkin. This is how
I loved you best, wrapped as a small gift to myself.
I woke up on a runway in New Orleans, steam rising
from the tarmac. The hurricane had passed. The city
a fazing wound wrapped in plywood and signal tape.
Humvees bivouacked down Canal Street, twisted
streetcar rails glistened in the sun-stained muck,
smeared shadows of the high-water mark
below the balconies on Esplanade Avenue.

You rounded the edges of my early middle years
when incidents accumulated in the shape of a tire fire.
I was housebound with a broken brain. I clawed
at the walls, left bits of flesh and fingernail
in the cracked plaster. Changed my mind,
but it was too late. This is how you found me.
We had shared friends, like the tonsured doctor
who soothed my simmering suspicions of you,
keeping us together for those long years until
the weight of his dissolution split the rotted
floor of his practice, leaving us homeless.

How I reached for you in the gray hours!
The sentinel of you on the nightstand,
a full magazine of perfect yellow bullets
and at the end a suicide spring outside
my living room window over the banks
of the same slow river 1,200 miles
north and a decade away at the center span
of the Franklin Avenue Bridge, which they tell me
is twelve stories up from the waterline without you
measuring the distance to solid ground.

Dr. Know

He doesn't look up from his laptop as he works
down his list of questions in a perfunctory clip.

Yet they are impossibly evocative these questions
(…interest or pleasure in doing things…? being
better off dead or…hurting..?) wrapped
in soft consonants and semi-vowels.

Your responses are warm gushes for air,
wet misshapen nuances of narrative
pouring over the ramparts of JavaScript.

Still, he will not look at you. So you search
the room for clues: a swath of downy dandruff
on his shoulder dappled in late morning
sunlight like the surface of a shimmering lake,
a soft place where you lay together on the shore.
His kiss comes as no surprise, though the plush
of his lips was more than you planned for,
the colloidal depth of his intention.

You leave with a slip of watermarked paper,
inscribed with the name of a small white pill.

It's what you came for. You will never see him again.

The Median

Scarred strands of scrub grass divide
the east-west lanes of the interstates crossing
this country. Seared by the sun, baked grey
by exhaust fumes, stained with shadowy
tidepools of brake fluid and engine oil
rinsed from the asphalt by rain.

Yet, there are northern places where the land
could not be flattened. The highway dips
and swags through tall timber. The median
widens with red oaks and sugar maples.
The ground is calmed by a carpet of wood ferns
and pine straw. Deep, still places moated
by asphalt, guarded by growling Peterbilts
pulling road trains that weave in the crosswind
like serpents.

The boy who peered from the passing car
would not be distracted by the rush and roar
of the road, or the cabin in the Adirondacks,
or the summer unfurling before him like honey,
or vistas of great European cities, or limitless
sweeps of white sand down the Kenyan coast.
None would sustain him as the years darkened,
the synapses crossed, the neurons misfired.

He learned to hide in plain sight. Yet he never
stopped staring into those small woods
wrapped in the clamorous interstate.
The impossible quiet of it all.

Something murmured from the soft forest floor.

Clinical

1.
Bindweed chokes the daylilies
in the side garden. We tear
it from the ground in clumps.
Its power lies not in its permanence,
but its persistence. Each morning,
new strands creep the mulch rows
like a wound that refuses to heal.
Diligence is all we have.

2.
I grew for seven years
before it came for me again,
cycling through medications
with the circling seasons like
a pharmaceutical fall color tour.
I measured the space between them
through a blossoming dripline.
The outer branches grew stronger.

3.
An errant neuron claws awake
in the subsoil, thirsting for serotonin
pooled in the cranial creek beds
after the dams were built. It's over
in the space of a dry season.
Seven years of cautious agronomy
abandoned to a riviera of silt.

Clinical, Part II

Daybreak arrives in the shape of a gun
and the scent of a white-hot headache.
The lindens bloom. The dog needs walking.
A west wind sweeps down from the Rockies
over the front range, though the Sandhills
to the salt marshes of eastern Nebraska
where the ponderosa pines arc with the strain
of it urging it onward over the Southlands
to the sea, where it sets me for a moment
on the foredeck of a ghost frigate, before
I slip overboard into the roiling deep.

Clinical Part III

Behind each eye is another eye.
The space within a cranial bulb
can't be described in dimensions:
Sinuous hills of grey, mottled
with knotweed and scrub pine
moored by a fallow sky. Not dark
not light. Nor day, nor night.

There was an incident
when I was a boy, followed
by a thousand more, as present
as the crow perched outside
my window. He calls
warnings to the house finches
gossiping around the feeder.
A Cooper's Hawk circles above.

A lifetime of humiliations hoarded
in the hippocampus. Some in
neat rows, some in sweaty piles.
The soul's claustral attic.
Everyone eyes the man,
few can see the ghost.

Clinical, Part IV

I can always tell, she says. It starts
when you can't look me in the eye.

It's true. A poorly kept secret
of a broken brain. We are left with
the company of objects low to the ground.
If you could see it, you would know
why we look away: the gnarled tip
of a claw roiling the milky sclera;
the raw edge of an animal trying
to shred its way out of its cranial cage.

If you could see it, you would recognize
the latched jaw, the grey strains of a visage
reduced to an inscrutable shadow.

Clinical, Part V

Not so much a screaking mandrake,
more like an ex-lover
yoked in coil, carting a bandsaw
or an ill-willed cousin.

Years wouldn't wrap you in Kevlar,
more like a cheap waistcoat,
a supermarket impulse buy:
a buttoned-up orange pill.

It comes with unlimited refills
in a discreet wrapper
ordered by a piebald jester
with a medical degree.

He is doing his best, of course.
No one promised a cure.
But this? This is a hammer claw
hacking through the cortex.

The neighbors mustn't be disturbed,
the small glands left alone
to pump the soup and goop that keeps
the weary corpus in tow.

Which brings us to the cruelest part:
the summing of same days,
a cawing covey of pleadings,
those only you can hear.

Clinical, Part VI

I arrive at a porous border
between the witching hour, a dream
from my perch on the quarter deck
on a freighter in the South China Sea,
tracing a body: naked, diaphanous
in the moon's bloom, wheeling
like a spindle in the dark water
until it is gone

and what comes in the day. An old man
in the south garden, bringing up rows
for the columbine, tearing at tentacles
of stickweed with slow shaking
fingers below skin leather gloves.

Both things become equally true
on a Tuesday morning, when the place
in the brain that cradles the soul
cracks. The amygdala scans
the living room for terror, and finds it.

Clinical, Part VII

Through a splintered lens, the mind's eye
muddles dawn and dusk. In this room
one checks the month, year to know
a life is passing. Somewhere
has to be a sturdy tool, a knife of
clean light to divvy night and day
in measured meter for the amygdala, orderly
pauses for neurons pulsing white-hot,
cradling demons swathed in shredded robes
of trauma worn from decades of wringing
over charred dendrites that carry the sour
smell of an electrical fire. Smoke crawls
through the louvers of the balcony door
in search of a passerby.

Clinical, Part VIII

Waiting for the medicine to cross
the blood-brain barrier, it's morning
on Interstate 57. A crack appears
in the new sky. A jackal's head pushes
through, smeared with vernix and slick.
Behind him are more jackals.

Waiting for the medicine to cross
the blood-brain barrier, a confab of
tinny voices crowd cochlear valleys.
Each is a memory, a humiliation
from yesterday or decades ago.
Behind them are more voices.

Waiting for the medicine to cross
the blood-brain barrier, the years
churl in a marish river twelve stories
down from a bridge where you were
already a ghost in a cranial floodplain.
Behind them are more years.

II

Dallas, 1978

For some, memory is a crowded construction site.
They pause with their children and speak
of what will be, marvel at the tower cranes
swinging steel beams like toys in the still summer
sky which is at once shapeless but formed,
limitless but lined.

Others see what was lost, histories in alleyways
and fried fish joints, a bramble of storefronts
where one could buy orange juice and cigarettes,
Mexican incense and Polish sausage.

When my brother split his knee on Peak Street
we thought the world would end.
I picked the glass out and wrapped the injury
in my tee. He took his shirt off too, and we belted
out 99 Bottles of Beer on the Wall as we stiff-legged
down Gaston Avenue for home, past the pawn shops
and jukebox bars where we would sometimes crack
a door and stare into the cool dark wanting
to fall into it, be taken by it, as if willing
our futures to be.

To the west, a late sun pooled on the skins
of new downtown skyscrapers. Some were still
shapes, unfinished puzzles of poured concrete
and steel that peered in disbelief (and later,
resolve) over those shabby streets.

The next year, I moved to Chicago with my mother.
He stayed behind with my father, who took him
out of East Dallas to a subdivision north of the city,
where new ranch homes were trimmed
with salvaged common brick from felled buildings

16

in cities like Toledo, Cleveland, and Detroit.
We traveled into manhood as strangers

where I struggle to remember the names
of his children who would not recall
an afternoon on Gaston Avenue when we shared
the same wound, in a city already forgetting
we were there.

Growing up Mao

One of the early objectives of the Cultural Revolution in China, which began in 1966 and goes on today, was to wipe out the "four olds"—old things, old ideas, old customs and old habits.
—Tillman Durdin. The York Times, May 19, 1971

Every Sunday night, my mother broiled a steak for my stepfather, the leader of the collective. She carried his meal (a thick, butter-soaked filet, extra rare, rivulets of blood pooling on an ivory-white plate, one of a set that was put aside just for him) to the master bedroom upstairs. The only room with an air conditioner, it was darkened with heavy drapes and a crimson rug. Under the bed were two loaded shotguns.

The house on Junius Street was a laboratory for a colloid of ideological strains carried over by the American Left as it lingered into the 1970s. It was a place of unremitting motion: community action meetings, rent strike rallies, food co-ops, free legal clinics, and donated toy giveaways for the neighborhood kids. Not for my brothers and sisters and me, though. We were assigned to sorting.

(On my ninth birthday, I received a miniature abacus decorated with a metal-plated Red Star along with a children's reader published by the foreign language press in Beijing—the story of a troop of city kids from the Youth League and the knowledge they gained on a trip to a collective farm in Shensi Province. That was the year my brother and I swiped skateboards from the toy giveaway. I still have mine.)

In the living room, vinyl-bound Little Red Books lay on the coffee table next to overfilled ashtrays. A framed section of a 1920s mural from the headquarters of the American Communist Party hung above the sofa. A dust-crusted Eugene Debs biography rested in a magazine tray next to one of the worn club chairs donated by the sociology department at El Centro Community College. Just out of law school attorneys and others my mother said were part of the movement lived with us. They fought and fucked in rooms down the hall. Journalists came calling, as did the FBI, the occasional narc, and the local PD.

Other grown-ups came and went, like the man who lived in the green house down the street. He gave karate lessons to boys on the block. We wouldn't tell my mother what happened there.

On Saturday afternoons, committees of the collective met in the dining room. We were forbidden to enter (except with cigarettes we lit on the stove for my mother) though we could hear raised voices muffled through the plaster walls, usually pleas and refutations of members who had come under scrutiny that week.

Towards the end of the decade, the lawyers left for cocaine and careers in the office towers going up on Commerce Street. My sisters' bodies changed, and my stepfather noticed. He left us for a 17-year-old who was pregnant by the time he filed papers. The police took the man in the green house away. My mother took a job at a real estate firm.

Our last summer there, my brother and I lit trashcans on fire. It would be years before I learned of the desecration of the Ming Tomb and the burning of the empress's bones, the ruin of Confucius's graveyard, or the sacking of the Temple of Heaven.

Though I had some knowledge by then, limited but useful from the year of my birth—the first chords of clarity in the jagged symphony of a boy's life, composed by the Great Leader's instructions to the Little Red Guards:

Sweep away the monsters and ghosts.

Eviction

On Eastlake Terrace, the contents of the apartment
are piled chest high on a thin strip of parkway
between the sidewalk and the curb. Things happened
in a hurry. The place looks scooped out by the armful:
an upturned nightstand in the ryegrass, a drawer
missing a dresser, filled with neatly balled socks,
a baby gate (perhaps for a puppy), a half-read copy
of The Thin Man, cut with a bookmark
from the Allentown book fair, the soft stuff of
indoor life, spread like viscera in the afternoon sun.

My brothers and sisters and me gathered fruit boxes
from behind grocery stores to pack our books
and bric-a-brac, mostly things important
only to a child: a Chinese abacus, a stuffed frog
that with our tired furniture would grow more bruised
with each journey. We would leave the mortally broken
things behind, prop a cleft table chair in the center
of a bare dining room, arrange torn paperbacks
on a makeshift windowsill bookshelf, stack
chipped cereal bowls neatly on the kitchen counter.

I came to understand the cover of nightfall,
my mother's boyfriend backing a creaky U-Haul
into the front yard at dusk. The neighbors must have
heard our hurried footsteps up the clanking load ramp,
and my mother's whispered instructions to hurry.
Did they watch from their windows, as the citizens
of Eastlake Terrace do now from the sidewalk,
moving slowly at first as crowds often do
towards the pile.

Obituary

for Alice Marie Smith

1.
Those of your kind that are left will line
the pews at First Presbyterian in blue Chanel
suits that hang from their spindly bodies
like Old Glory on a windless January day.
They will cough politely, be assisted
by their sixty year old children, cry
tears of dust and aerosol.

2.
1942. His P-47 falls into the ocean. He writes
from a field hospital in Samoa. The atoll was
shark infested, his face and chest
hammered into the pull stick, blood
and the rest of it left behind as he crawls
from his wrecked ship. A long, soundless
night save for the tumble of the sea and his
chanting the sweetheart's name he gave you
at Lake Texoma in the summer of '39. It kept him
alive. He left a son with you. You would see
his face there. And you would seethe.

3.
The Reverend Tyler Johnson will officiate, but you will direct.
The local mortician will do you up nice, pry
the last smirk from your lips, fold your lank fingers
over a frigid patch of skin where your heart
used to be. There will be thin eulogies that dissolve
in the air above the rafters. Your curriculum
vitae will be read between the lines of names
and places like Gate City, Virginia, United Daughters
of the Confederacy, Order of the Eastern Star,

Daughters of the American Revolution.
No one in that fearful crowd will afford the irony
of a woman so vainglorious of her ancestry,
yet so repulsed by those
whose ancestry she will be.

4.
1967. You sent toy guns for Christmas.
My mother threw them away.
Tet the following year.

5.
1993. We met once, you and me. At my father's funeral.
We shook hands. We shook hands. The sum total
of us.

6.
When November comes in North Texas
not so much as a quail will stir around your grave.
Toss a hand of dry dirt over the coffin, boys.
Watch it sift over the cool mahogany

and fall away.
Nothing ever grew there.
Nothing ever will.

Jimmy Stevens

The winter of 1976 set records in North Texas. Water pipes froze under the crumbling cotton mansions in East Dallas. My mother took a hair dryer into the crawl space, the whites of her eyes lit the dark beneath my feet as I peered through the round hole in the dining room floor where decades earlier an electric call button sat. With the tap of a foot, the cook could be summoned from the kitchen, or the maid who had been dusting the nursery. I would spend hours in that dining room, tapping my foot over that hollow spot in the floor, conjuring servants to help me solve such problems of powered milk and twenty cent loaves of white bread. Had they come, they would have called out to their employers at the sight of me, the second-hand bunk beds in the sunroom, pockmarked corona tiles on the Spanish roof, spider-veined sidewalks. Ours was a migrant's fear – white families, whose poverty lingered through generations like an unyielding strand of DNA; African American families moving north from the neighborhoods below the fairgrounds; Latino families, whose fathers and uncles roasted goats in backyards on Worth Street and fed the block birria on Easter. Even the hippies, aging and strung out on amphetamines, envisaged their return: clans of good Baptists and Presbyterians stepping across the years as if they were puddles along the curb after a rainstorm -- glaziers, electricians, and policemen in tow -- to reclaim their stately homes. Even the imagined rich had power over us.

At least we had coats, though they were too thin for that kind of winter. Jimmy Stevens was the first kid I saw without one. We were walking in packs down Gaston Avenue for Davy Crockett Elementary. Jimmy's arms were crossed in a self-embrace under a worn windbreaker. His gloveless hands were a reddish blue. "Forgot my coat," he said with an uneasy laugh as he weaved quickly through clumps of us, trying to space some distance. Though as he got past one cluster, he'd come up on another group of boys, slow-moving freighters to Jimmy's scampering sampan.

Still, even the meanest of them didn't say anything. We all knew how close we were. We would take our proximity to Jimmy Stevens to a place where none could find it, even ourselves.

I would like to believe that I am different, that I recalled Jimmy Stevens in a righteous moment: a communion wafer on my tongue, or as a response to that colleague who only sees such scarcity through the privileged lens of academic theory.

But it wasn't so. Jimmy Stevens came back to me on a February morning in the parking lot of a Hampton Inn outside of Aberdeen, South Dakota. The cold tore through me, stripped the dross and dressing we wrap around memory until it becomes something else or nothing at all. I had filled the space of youth with a rigid refusal that became my own gospel. Though gaps in the doxology revealed themselves in ways that could still extract a toll all those decades later: my geometry teacher telling me in front of the class that he tried to call my house the night before, but the phone was disconnected. Or Lydia Fallon in the cafeteria line, telling me with a saccharine smile that I must really like that shirt because I sure wear it a lot.

What became of you, Jimmy Stevens? Though I know you wanted me to, I am sorry I looked away. The price I paid was a steep one. I hope you found some warmth in your life, that a quiet smile breaks over your lips as you wrap your own children for a January morning when they complain their coats are too heavy, their gloves are too thick.

Billy

In the early 1970s, every summer my mother removed the middle seat and issued each of us a milk crate (only what fits, she said) she liberated from the loading dock of the Tom Thumb on Preston Avenue. The next morning, we headed west for California. To keep the questions and the predators away, she would tack a notice on the bulletin board at the Y for a man to share the driving in exchange for the ride. I remember Billy the best. My sisters said he was queer and a prostitute and a hustler. When money ran low, we pulled into a truck stop with a motel attached. Billy returned the next morning and we left in a hurry. We bought groceries in the next town.

This my mother called freedom. Crossing Death Valley in a VW microbus. Summers in a rented flat in the Haight. Needle addicts in the alley, a six-foot high cannabis called "Baby" in the bay window, Black Panther rallies, anti-war rallies, six-year-olds handing out leaflets with pictures of political prisoners. For years I struggled to know what she used for chains, and why we were made accessories in her escape. In the food stamps and hand-me-down clothes years that followed, I rejected the bony lap of others' misery.

Billy, though. Billy didn't need to conjure devils. For a man like him, they were everywhere. I learned from my mother, but Billy was my teacher.

The Last Time

This is where they always fought,
an unlit corner of the K-mart parking lot.
She'd left him again. Though he always knew
where to find her. In the witching hour.

Seven children shaken out of bed, caged
in a VW microbus. It was August
the last time. Soaked in fear, and sweat,
and waiting. Fevered whispers. Mostly silence

as he pulls up behind us, his high beams
shear the private shadows from our faces.
He rips his keys. The engine gurgles.
Firing staccato of his Justins over the asphalt.

She left the driver's door unlocked, a dark game
of trust they played. She may have known
there would be no rules this time.
He wrenches her from the car by her hair.

After, her bruised fingers on the wheel.
Then the gift: a right turn on Hall Street.
Home was left. This is where they always fought,
an unlit corner of the K-mart parking lot.

A Mother's End

In an old house
overlooking a dead lake
she draws the blinds on summer days
to keep the sunlight at bay.

She's kept company by an old dog
who lays unstirring on the floor
save for the momentary heaving
of his tattery breathing.

There is a radio on in every room.
The mellow monotone of strangers
a lullaby to the dander and dust
swaddling the furniture like rust.

There were children about, and are still,
who cannot unwrap her surrender
to know if there was dignity this way,
this flinty fading away.

Orange County

The young cardiac surgeon is practically giddy
with a report that he rebuilt my mother's heart.
He stands over the clutch of us, withered
on a faux leather couch slicked with paste
of dried tears and body smells of others' grief
before us. I have images, he says
turning his phone towards us like a 7th grader
clasping a ribbon from the middle school science fair.
The first is a shadowy pool of white, ridged
with thin black lines that taper to filigree
in the ether until they disappear like ghosts.
In the second, those same black lines bold,
swollen with new blood like snowmelt rushing
through a desert riverbed in early spring.
Scrubbers and scrapers had cleared decades
of fibrin and Winston Lights from her arteries.
There was talk of the long road ahead.

I couldn't shake the vanity from it. My sisters
making the sign of the cross. An 81-year-old
heart and all it carried made to plough on.
She would be dead within the hour.
Paddle jolts and the crush of compressions
made a knotted junk heap of the chromium alloy
and medical-grade stainless steel in her chest.

The young surgeon had already departed.
Off to Irvine to perform another miracle.

Passage

As a bargain for her life, bridled by demons
she conjured, others she indulged, and all we bore
witness to, I prayed only that my mother
be accorded comfort and dignity in her death.
She received neither. When they called for paddles,
I left the room.

In the fifty-three minutes she lived
after the surgery my mother raged. Refused.
Blood ran down my brother's arm as she tore
at her IVs. Restraints were ordered. Nurses harried
to stanch the catheter wounds in her legs. Technicians
ministered whizzing pumps like mechanics trying
to unchoke a seizing engine amid a cacophony
of electronic alerts and urgent orders.

She cried out for dead people as if they were
huddled there in the corner of the room hoping
not to be seen. She quieted when she had their attention.
Things were said. Some unspeakable things.
She spoke them.

The compressions were violent, atavistic. Her body
buckled. Ribs cracked like reedy bone being torn apart
by a larger animal in a forest field. The cardiologist's eyes
said thank you when my sister called an end to it.

A milquetoast chaplain arrived at the bedside and read
a generic poem for the dead from his iPhone. My sister
dismissed him. I quarried what I could from Psalm 23
from memory, searching the room for clues.
Through a slit window, two tugs drew a cargo ship
into Long Beach Harbor. To still waters her leads me.

There was no nimbus in the re-circulated air, nor ether
hovering in the ballast of the overhead fluorescents. We
were denied the thinnest thread from which we could stitch
hopeful revisions in the narrative of the fifty-three minutes
that bookended my mother's life. She shared nothing
save for a hint. The tight smirk she wore
in her waking years was missing. My mother
died with her mouth open. For a woman whose
life was scraping of flint against ragged rock,
here it was: a perfect oval. The shape of wonder
at what only she could see.

Reckoning

There were no light shapes in the room
where my mother had passed.
Though there was silence, which was new
after hours of pleading.

Not us. We were well-prepared.
We'd lived her memories,
the ones crashing through the rampart
hewn over jagged years.

As each stone fell, there was terror
of course, and something else.
Protest at first, then a whisper.
An atonement. Perhaps.

More likely a soul unready
for this. For reckoning.
To decipher at the moment
her life came true.

Still, we sang to her at the end
as one would to a child.
Parents learn to soothe the restive.
Spells we taught each other.

Western Auto

Here's a scent that demands recall,
fresh rubber drifting over the stalls of new
road bikes at Walmart. We patched tires on
Huffy tires with kits from Western Auto. All

we needed for our getaways, the fires
we rode from those summers. Mired
with my brother in things barely known.
It was a boy's life, wrapped by a lady

who settled for the unquiet side
of his mind, payment
for all those years without a man.
We were there, yet she was alone.

We swore we'd unlearn it. Though the plan
was flawed. Our demands were formless
and mute. The women who came gave
what we needed, more than we deserved.

As it is now is as it was then, in an echo
where we find ourselves men.

III

Ritual

Two AM on the Las Vegas Strip at the steps of the Tropicana overpass. A Guatemalan family passes out flyers for escort services and all-male reviews. I am holding a red apple in my left hand which I will bite into as I cross the casino floor at the Palazzo, as is my ritual on my last night here.

The flight home was violence. Cataracts of clotted lightening off the starboard wing. I heard the usual intercessions one relies on in these moments. Hurried Our Fathers swirled fore and aft in the recirculated air until they became a fevered invocation among us, something like a chant in the trembling firmament over Moorhead, Minnesota.

Perhaps that's what put us there, pilgrims in that shuddering 737. Instructions from St. Ignatius's Instructions to query the Holy Spirit as to what God thinks is particularly important. Were we surprised that it wasn't the pitch of the wings, or the flight attendant making the sign of the cross as he straps into the jump seat, or at that very moment, even us?

Liver cancer dissolves the boyhood friend of the man in 23C. The woman in 18F recalls an ill word spoken to her by her mother twenty years ago. A twelve-year-old boy crosses a desert to slip a glossy image of a man wearing a top hat and star-spangled bikini briefs into my one free hand.

Mr. Katz in Wartime

Last summer, the Japanese beetles took what was left
of the yews guarding the old Tudor on Aldrich Road.

Mr. Katz keeps watch from his lawn chair.
They put a bronze star on him 70 years after the war.

Mr. Katz told me the story of the Arkansas Brigade
as he instructed me on the importance of poisoning
the sumac creeping up on the lilac and bloodroot
in the side yard. It's been there for a long time.
It's just hard to see.

I bet you didn't know there were Southern boys
manning Fort Kearney during the war.

Captured Confederates from Johnson's Island
dispatched to the Indian Frontier. Issued rifles,
artillery, and a government guarantee
not to be sent south to fight their brothers
in the uniform of their new army.
They were called Galvanized Yankees.
History does not tell what they called themselves.

By late afternoon, Mr. Katz dozes off
beneath a canopy of red oak and ponderosa pine,
and the years that leave shadows before us.

Mr. Katz Dreaming (The Sheet Cake Lady Prayer)

The night nurse's Subaru rests
on the blacktop driveway Mr. Katz
and his sons poured in 1979, beneath
the one-hundred-year-old pin oak
Mr. Katz has kept alive for the past
ten years with spikes filled with an iron
drip, and splints hemming the drowsy
low limbs that rasp in newborn winds.

He just sleeps now, through the dry days
of Nebraska winter. The last time
we spoke, after the operation he said
shot his nerves all to hell, he described
his hallucinations to me. She comes to him
in the afternoons, a dark-haired woman
with skin the color of sheet cake.
She visits with me. I set out a chair
for her next to mine in the garage.

I yearn to see him again, to ask
him what he sees with his eyes
closed: a sliver of sunlight through
the knotted branches of a banyan tree
glinting the scope of his sniper's rifle,
blood drying on a beach in Guam,
the tracing arc of an American Century
he couldn't have seen coming in those
moments. Would he call it peace?
It happened so fast. The rubble
of empires. ICBMs trenched
across the Northern Plains. Firehoses
on the streets of Birmingham.
Skylines turned to gravelly dust.

Let it be Sheet Cake Lady.
Place her soft hand on his shoulder
as the pin oak sighs a seraphic surrender
as the splints and rods slip free.

A House in Lincoln

A penny an acre, as history tells
The Pawnee received when made forced to sell.
The railroad got it for far even less,
Free in due fact from a deep public well.

The trains came through and on they pressed,
Then sold the extra land in a claim of redress
For the risk they bore to build this new State,
A junction at Kearney and every point west.

For forty more years the land lay in wait
Until this Tudor was built in red brick and slate.
Financed in a Trust the Union Bank would seed
On a one-acre lot with a wrought iron gate.

The new house came with a plain-worded deed.
Whites Only it said, though there was hardly a need.
None different were left, as for the Pawnee
I hold a mortgage with an overdue fee.

Native Grass

By August, only the hardiest grasses
will have pulled through. But this is
early spring, and the soil is crawling
with malcontents. Plush loam lays
unguarded against the invasives.
Creeping mobs of catsfoot and thistle
lay siege to the bluestem and dropseed
just rising from spongy root beds
after a long Nebraska winter.

By May, prowling knotweed lays
a veneer of smothering sap green over
the wild places. By July, what's left of
the natives are curated in vanity gardens
and ornamental parkways fronting
the government buildings on K Street.

Meanwhile, a blue-eyed boy sips
a 32-ounce Mountain Dew Liberty Brew®
in the Flying J parking lot outside of Kearney.
His gaze is westward. It's Destiny.

Natives

A sod cutter the color of a roadwork sign
coughing black smoke from a gummed up
carburetor slices three inches of topsoil
from Mrs. K's filet-sized yard, pushing
the amputated slabs, corpuscled with blue
violet and wild phlox to a flatbed idling

at the curb. We're bringing back the natives
says Mrs. K, as the thick man-master of
the cutting machine loads up for his next client
a few houses down in this leafy neighborhood
of law professors and staff accountants
to remake their parcels into a past before

we arrived, before the university down
the street with its tribal-named football team
and the robber baron's estate outside of town
with its public gardens walled with mossy
palisades for peonies and French daisies guarded
by Siamese Buddhas and Greco-Roman fetishes.

The finches and rodents go about their work
laying hints in the soil as to where history
dwells, starlings drive the swallows out of
their cavities in the pin oaks and the blue jay
mimics the cry of the hawk to plunder fledglings
from the oriole's nest, neverminding his conquest.

When the clearing is done, the man-master lays
a synthetic straw net over Mrs. K's yard
to keep the rain from running off with the seed.

Home on the Plains

Beneath decades of flooring,
pine planks smeared with glue,
asbestos, linoleum, stick-on tile,
there is a hatch. You pry it open
with a crowbar and a scrape.
Beneath the hatch is a crawlspace
one only enters if something is dire.
A burst pipe. A nest of bull snakes.
History. We'd rather not know

what's soughing in the cold dirt.
Until it comes for us. Then we know.

New Year's Eve in Chicago

He hides in his little room.

> the one in the back
> of the apartment

> away from her.

They have parties.

> two glasses of champagne,
> and china from France.

> where they spend some time.

He hides in his little room.

> with his law degree,
> and his dandruff shampoo.

They have parties.

> and give me thirty dollars,
> to wash their dishes.

> the ones from France.

Where they spend some time.

The Man Across the River in Saint Paul

There is a man across the river who swears he knows me, perched over a picnic table mottled with bird droppings and last bits of melting snow. I'm a stranger here myself, though he seems intent on selling this business. He waves both arms for me to approach, like a flagman. The least I can do is acknowledge the semaphore, so I my wave my hand slowly in a crawling arc from left to right. A coffin-black gravel barge slips into the frame. The man across the river disappears from view. When the barge has passed the man is gone. There's a smell of diesel in the wake. I'm left in the slow rolling, just beneath the surface of ice-green water.

Home

We were furthest away from home
that long season after middle age.
We are childless. One of those couples
people whisper about at cocktail parties,
proffering hushed hypotheses.

The cities became intolerable,
lapped in light and boulevards
shuttling futures in the afternoon rush.
We wanted for narrowing roads
wandering dusk-smoked hills.

In hard water country, runnels of dew
seep through the marl, leaving elegant
skeletons etched in stone foundations.
Watery wind spills from the Rockies,
kilns over the high desert.

By eastern Nebraska, smoothed
by grasslands and diamond willows,
it feels like funeral silk draped
under a new pine: a place to grow
old together, but not alone.

After Cancer
(Cherry County, Nebraska)

The light shines in the darkness, and the darkness has not overcome it.
—John 1:5

Hillsides painted in fan strokes of autumn
bluestem and Indian grass. At dusk, shadows
crawl through the shallow valleys.
We were left with sloping giants
under a lantern of Orion and a setting Venus.
A coyote howls.

On the way up, I lit a candle at St. Anselm's
(the marquee says "The Cathedral of the Sandhills!")
in memory of memory.

We never touched, though we embraced.
You said, "the hills have the last word."
A whisper, really. Unheard by time.
Satin symphony of light and shadow.
Something eternal came true.

Travelers

So much for the slowness of the thing.
Though there were sweet seasons, the mossy
green of her eyes like a velvet woodland floor
where one could take a rest as we did
that September afternoon, pulling off a stretch
of the New York Thruway, hiking into a deep
grove of sugar maples and silver birch.
We made love in a sateen of leaf litter
as the semis geared down in the distance.

The years pass and the body reveals more.
A still shape suspended in a dim, watery place.
Filigree of root dislodge from tenuous soil,
then fall away into the dark. On instructions
we collected the tissue. You can use a kitchen strainer,
said the obstetrician, who was awkward as we were
pulling at embryonic pieces with rubber-tipped tongs
stained with milk of Michigan cherries and overripe plums.

Things were breaking all around us that summer.
The house rebelled in a series of small complaints.
Face nails squirmed free from the floorboards. A frayed
sash cord snapped from its pulley and disappeared
into the inscrutable innards of a window frame.
A strap hinge dislodged from the backyard gate, twitching
on its slip post, unaware of its own brokenness, creaking
psalms in the autumn wind. Scarlet oaks moaned replies.

There were final scenes, more than a few. An echo
in a San Francisco hotel room, perhaps for no other reason
than it was San Francisco, or a corporeal praise song
to outlast the fear that we were becoming mirror images
of one another's loss, which isn't really loss because you are
always left with something. For us, it was a few years

later still. In a cabin outside of Whitefish, Montana.
It is late autumn. A parchment of snow skims the sagebrush,
hushing the grey foothills. The sheets fall away.
Her gaze is already past me, towards the dry dusk
to settle for a fresh set of stars to guide the way.

The Suit

Mrs. Kim's eyes rise slowly from the fabric
to meet his. She is old as well, her body
crooked from years over a stitching machine.
The garment carousel whirs on its serpentine track.
Work shirts and cocktail dresses filled with light
and air mingles in the space above. A late
summer sun sifts through the dust that mottles
the shop windows, laying a patchwork of light
on the scuffed linoleum floor, like gossamer
through the apostles in the clerestory windows
at Chartres where my sister and I wandered
with pilgrims and tourists that difficult summer,
her at the end of her marriage, me already
with the knowing what would become
of my only child, undisturbed and innocent
in the yawning dark of transition.

The man carefully lays a dark blue suit over the counter.

May I have this suit back by Tuesday morning?

How are you? How your wife?

She passed away yesterday.

A delivery truck gears down on Asbury Avenue,
rattling the shop door. Something rustles
behind a fitting room curtain.

Yes. Tuesday. And no charge for you, Mr. Lewis, she says.

You already pay.

Disagreement

When it was winter,
you laid down. I stood up
backed away from an empty bed
and whirled into the night.

I returned at dawn.
You doubted my rebirth.
Though I was smeared in vernix,
slickened with new ideas

from a womb of middle years.
Something we crawl from
not for light the newborn knows,
but for knowledge of the end,

the way to it. What shocked me
was how little you would settle for.
As if this were a small concern,
this low ache, this slow turn

away from the corpus.
Memory will glaze it
you say, like a soft patina
for the bronze of our age.

There is still a storm! Righteous
tumble of thunder, lightning
and plush rain after. We are that
liquid and light. Not still,

not yet.

Homecoming

1.

The best part about clearing customs at O'Hare was the steel doors at the end of the long corridor and the sea of sound and color on the other side. Homemade signs held in the hands of entire families who cheered as they caught sight of the relative they had saved for years to bring over, like Dominik down the block on Argyle Street who added another room to the bungalow with the arrival of each brother. By the end of the decade, the house was a contraption (my brother called it Rancho Polonia) and something of a local tourist attraction in our corner of Albany Park. But it was our contraption, and we revered it like a castle on a hill.

2.

It was usually the end of September and a girl waiting for me. I would see her first, cheering with a Chinese family like they were her own. Who wouldn't want to be caught up in this? As if we too were fresh with new country and I had escaped the apparatchiks and black markets with only a Jansport touring pack and a few pieces of indeterminate currency at the end of the American Century.

3.

We would start our new life together that afternoon under a blanket of scarlet oaks in the bedroom of her 4th floor apartment on Surf Street. High leaves already signaled autumn and days we would spend lurking galleries and museums or hiking abandoned factories on Cermak Road, our Nikon lenses trained on the intangible past of others mingling with our futures beneath a canopy of uncluttered years.

4.

A quarter of a century later after a late flight from Mexico City a familiar flutter of anticipation with a push on a steel door, a tug on the sleeve of memory from an old friend perhaps trying to get a message to me -- to soften the edges of November, an early winter, this ragged lobby I step into, empty save for a security guard who picks his nose beneath a soundless television monitor and a weary livery driver in a dusty black suit who wears a yarmulke and holds a sign that reads the name of a Spanish fertilizer company. The flight crew fans past me, cool and indifferent to time and geography, their rollaboards popping staccato over the rock salt speckling the terrazzo at the curbside doors.

5.
In the taxi line, a man asks me how was my journey. It doesn't occur to me that he is a stranger.

Debris

-after Air France Flight 447

On our nightstands, we place small devices
that keep watch on our world as we sleep.
We fear turning them off at night
lest we lose track of things, the narrative of
our lives compressed into packets, swirling
in the grey air between relay antennas
affixed to chimney rises of shuttered factories
at the edges of once great cities.

I knew a woman, an obstetrician, who wanted
her tombstone to read I wasn't here.

For some children, the chaos around them is
so unreal it seems imaginary. They have little
use for aphorism and make-believe. This is how
I came to reject a world with four corners.
Though I knew what a circle is if not a square.
These are children you should not fuck with.

Meanwhile, search planes from the world's
mightiest navies stitch grids over a distant sea
aided by satellites so powerful they can recognize
a mole on a human face. But there is no debris,
nor the dimmest signal from any machine.

The hardest thing is this. For the weary
weight of us, the howling mess of us,
the world can still summon the means to silence us,
pull us beyond reach of ourselves.

Would you deny it, felled there in a soundless sea?
Would you cry out, I was here!
Or would you consider, at that last moment,
perhaps you never were.

What the Block Was Made For

The next-door neighbor is going for father of the year. These past three weekends, he and his boys play superhero games in homemade capes. I watch from the kitchen window which at this moment I notice has a hairline crack veining from the mortise joint in the lower sash.

In the next room is a woman who has loved me for 20 years. We are childless. One of those couples people talk about in certain company, proffering hushed explanations for misfortune. Like losing an arm in a farm accident. Or being born without legs.

A little girl and her mother pin baskets on the porch where Mr. Poleski used to smoke Chesterfields through the afternoon. There's a Slip 'N Slide in the yard where Kim serenaded her aging poodle to coax a bony stream of urine from his withered bladder. When he'd finished, he'd labor back inside to his ragged spot at the end of the couch and settle in for the rest of the day to dream old dog dreams, occasionally raising a slow eye to investigate the sound of a delivery truck passing, or a bare branch scraping. This was a block made for autumn and evening, bounded by drift and routine.

Not a dewy morning in June swaddled in soft air and peals of discovery, chipping the dusty mortar, rattling the spalled bricks.

After 50

After 50, the stumbling years reappear with fresh fury. There was no censure then, nor was there praise. The streets were glossed with rain. There was only sightless beauty, a bloodshot groping. On a boat to Brindisi, a boy on the edge of manhood believes he is alone in a body of strangers, all inseparably beautiful. He gives in to it. He continued like this for many years. He suffered indignations at regular intervals for the gilded cult of himself. He stood for nothing. It was for nothing that he stood. The brave boast boundless compassion. It is only the coward who cannot forgive the bully. After 50, lichen squeeze the oxygen out of the lake. The amygdala sends up signal flares. It's the surrender he will miss the most, the sum of a thing so much more than you.

Clark Street Sonnet

There are myriad paths to memory.
One is winter, driving north on Clark Street
on a February night, mysteries
rising from the pavement like steam, to greet

me where I grew, howling the alleyways
and other jagged places, secret maps
of these neighborhoods, where I gladly paid
the bargain price of youth, in a basement flat

with a dime bag and luck. We groped out loud
though we knew the place was changing, in pursuit
of new gentry, condos, a money crowd
in us, around us, emptying of youth.

Yet these streets stayed with me, what I became,
still in the shadows, reinventing the game.

On Summit Avenue

Snow on the sugar maples this morning.
Eleanor doesn't like the looks of it,
which might be as far as this poem goes
were it not for the powder gathering
on the late autumn leaves like spoonfuls
of cake. It's a mystery how we slipped
into middle age like this: mutual funds
and pet medications shrouded in squishy
canine treats. Also, sweetheart, you snore.
Has anyone ever told you that? No matter.
We'll be home before the wind dies down.
Our autumns have become our springs.
Shimmering ryegrass, a filigree of bronze
draped over the oaks on Summit Avenue.
How lovely they are to be older than we.

An Ending

As we rounded an inlet past Sturgeon Bay
two piping plovers cried warnings, enough
to call a nearby nest to keep away
from a Cooper's Hawk that shot from the bluff
to take one of the plovers as it flew
above the water's edge. She drowned the bird
between two stones in a tide pool. We knew
the quick work hawks make of these things, had heard
sound before dying before. How could we
have prepared for the stubborn silence
of an underwater end? Now unfree,
we railed against it, though the violence
fueled our reaching that night before the fire.
Flesh ages, though the body still desires.